Red-Letter Day
DEVOTIONAL

JAMES W. REED III

ISBN 979-8-88540-530-0 (paperback)
ISBN 979-8-88540-531-7 (digital)

Christian Faith Publishing
832 Park Avenue
Meadville, PA 16335
www.christianfaithpublishing.com

Printed in the United States of America

Acknowledgments

I truly believe no significant accomplishment in life is ever achieved alone. Of course, we recognize God's hand in everything, and I thank Him for every page of my life. I believe He brings and places people in our lives to serve as an inspiration, coach, influence, supporter, and, most of all, an expression of His love. So I thank God for Pamela, my wife; Kameron and James IV, my sons; and Toni, Linda, Patsy, and Lonnie, my siblings, for all their love, inspiration, influence, and support.

I also want to acknowledge the Rising Sun Baptist Church family for your love and support. It is these God-placed people who have made this accomplishment and journey so very special and rewarding. Thank you!

Preface

In 2020, at the height of the pandemic, I remember asking myself the question, will it ever get any better? Because each day seemed to bring more bad news. There were times I didn't think I would make it. The walls, the world seemed as if they were closing in on me, and I couldn't catch my breath. I would talk to God about my feelings, and He would remind me of who I was, the son of the Most High. Even with that, the struggle continued.

As the days and weeks went by, I noticed something about myself. Each day, all day, I found myself talking to the Lord about my feelings. Not that I didn't talk to the Lord before, but these conversations were different. Many times, we talk to God simply to complain, make a request, or get a quick answer to a problem. But these conversations had become a desperate need to hear His calming voice. During this time, I was having many conversations with people about what was going on, trying to help calm their fears. All along within myself, anxiety was building. But the daily conversations with the Lord got me through a moment, then a day, and then a week. I found myself so reliant on those conversations, which is exactly where God wanted me.

By year's end, I had a sense of calm, new perspective, different priorities, and purpose. But the new year picked up where the past one ended. A siege on our nation's capital, a crippling freeze, and the pandemic still raging, but my calm remained. This was when the reality of what got me through was on center stage. God gave me this word:

> The steps of a man are established by the
> Lord, and He delights in his way. When he falls,
> he will not be hurled headlong, because the Lord
> is the One who holds his hand. I have been young
> and now I am old, yet I have not seen the righ-

teous forsaken or his descendants begging bread.
(Psalms 37:23–25)

That when we trust God each day for direction, we can have the calm of knowing no matter how bad it gets, the Lord is holding our hand through it all, and we will survive. I realized that those daily conversations with God, sharing my feelings and hearing His voice, got me through. That is what inspired this devotional. I truly believe having a daily conversation with God will bring the calm and purpose to each day. I trust that this devotional will give you the opportunity to experience what I did in the midst of a difficult year.

Red-Letter Day Devotional

A red-letter day typically denotes a day that is pleasantly noteworthy, memorable, or of special significance. With that in mind, I cannot think of any other day that is or would be more noteworthy or significant than a day that starts with talking to and/or hearing from GOD.

David wrote,

> The steps of a man are established by the Lord, and He delights in his way. When he falls, he will not be hurled headlong, because the Lord is the One who holds his hand. I have been young and now I am old, yet I have not seen the righteous forsaken or his descendants begging bread. (Psalms 37:23–25)

In other words, each day and in each circumstance, one should talk to or hear from the Lord, that one can walk confidently, knowing that should he or she stumble the Lord Himself will uphold him or her. Therefore, each day concludes with a testimony of no regrets.

The red letters of the Bible are the words and promises spoken only by the Lord. The apostle Paul, John, and James, all inspired by God, shared great and mighty words, but these next sixty days of inspirational devotion come only from the words of the Lord. I pray that you will take this sixty-day journey with the Lord, allowing Him to speak to you each day and grow into a more intimate relationship with Him. As you listen to Him the first thirty days, you will have the opportunity to respond by journaling your prayer each day. The second thirty days will give you each day the opportunity to journal what you hear God saying in the Scriptures and your response to Him in prayer. Make the next sixty days a red-letter day each day!

Day 1

Follow Me, and I will make you become fishers of men.

—Mark 1:17

Jesus has begun His day and ministry along the Sea of Galilee. He sees the fishermen, Simon and Andrew, casting their nets. Jesus invites them to follow Him, and He would change their priorities, direction, and occupation. Our jobs, our priorities, and directions are typically the foundation of our lives. But as we see, Jesus brought a significant change in the life of these men who chose to follow Him. He wants to do the same for us.

So we should always be prepared to hear from the Lord. Each day that we begin with prayer and devotion gives God our ear to hear from Him. Too often we set our course for the day and ask God to bless it but spend extraordinarily little time seeking His direction. Jesus teaches us to take time each day to hear what God is saying; it will surely make a significant change in your life.

What is your prayer concerning what Jesus said to you?

_____

_____

_____

_____

_____

_____

_____

_____

_____

_____

Day 2

It is written, "Man shall not live on bread alone, but on every word that proceeds out of the mouth of God."

—Matthew 4:4

Jesus had been led into the wilderness by the Spirit to be tempted by the devil. After forty days of fasting, the devil challenges the Lord to turn stones into bread. Jesus's response was that there are more important choices in His life. Jesus chose the word and will of God over human needs and desires. What was offered to Jesus was not something that He did not need or want, nor was it wrong. He chose what was most important in His particular circumstance.

The reality is that we all at some point must make choices. Jesus reminds us not to allow physical conditions to push us into choosing comfort and desire over the word and will of God.

What is your prayer concerning what Jesus said to you?

_____

_____

_____

_____

_____

_____

_____

_____

_____

_____

_____

Day 3

You shall worship the Lord your God and serve Him only.

—Luke 4:8

Ambition, accomplishment, and achievement are things to be admired. Jesus is offered a bargain that would cost Him His allegiance to God. Jesus quickly acknowledged that the price was much too high.

Often because of the subtleties of the offer, we sell our allegiance for the things that we most admire and desire. Ambition, accomplishment, and achievement are admirable qualities but only at the right price. Our allegiance and relationship to God is nonnegotiable, and we should nurture it as such through our worship and obedience to the will of God. Jesus reminds us to love Him with all our heart, mind, and soul…

What is your prayer concerning what Jesus said to you?

_____
_____
_____
_____
_____
_____
_____
_____
_____
_____

Day 4

It is said, "You shall not put the Lord your God to the test."

—Luke 4:12

In an attempt to deceive Jesus, by misinterpreting scripture (Psalms 91:11–12) Satan would be changing God's timing and plan. Jesus had confidence that God was with Him and that His Father's plan and timing were perfect. Jesus didn't fall for Satan's deception.

When we try to shortcut or alter God's plan, we in essence are telling God we don't trust Him. Regardless of our circumstance, God is to be trusted. As we approach each day, always remember the words spoken by the prophet Jeremiah from God:

> For I know the plans that I have for you, declares the Lord, plans for welfare and not for calamity to give you a future and a hope. (Jeremiah 29:11 NASB)

Don't allow the deception of our circumstances to cause us to test God. We simply need to stand on the promises of God and trust His perfect timing and plan. Jesus is telling you, don't test Him but trust Him.

What is your prayer concerning what Jesus said to you?

_____
_____
_____
_____
_____
_____
_____

Day 5

Before Philip called you, when you were under the fig tree, I saw you.

—John 1:48

Nathanael asked Jesus a question. "How do you know me?" That could be the question we all ask. Jesus saw Nathanael setting under a fig tree. He reminded Nathanael that He saw him before he came looking for Him.

It is comforting to know that Jesus sees us no matter where we are or what our circumstance or condition may be. He sees us setting under our fig tree trying to figure life out. He sees the single mom, the grieving mother, the struggling student, the jobless man, the sickly neighbor, and, yes, even you who may be stuck in a bad relationship.

A sobering thought: we don't have to wait on Jesus; He is waiting on us. When it is so easy to get lost in obscurity, there is the comfort of knowing that Jesus is saying to us all, *"I see you."* What an awesome thought to live by…

What is your prayer concerning what Jesus said to you?

_____

_____

_____

_____

_____

_____

_____

_____

_____

Day 6

I am the Light of the world, he who follows Me will not walk in the darkness, but will have the Light of life.

—John 8:12

At the very beginning of time, God declared that there be light. Light represented the presence, power, and guidance of God. Jesus now declares Himself to be that light of the world. He then promises that those who would follow Him would not walk in darkness, that is to walk alone, operate in our human weakness, and live with no purpose or direction. But the promise was that we would live in the presence of God, operate in and through the awesome power of God, and have our steps ordered by the guidance of God. As we approach each new day, Jesus reminds us that no matter how dark the days may become, if we follow Him, we will walk in the light of life, the very presence, power, and guidance of God.

What is your prayer concerning what Jesus said to you?

_____

_____

_____

_____

_____

_____

_____

_____

_____

Day 7

Behold, an Israelite indeed, in whom there is no deceit!

—John 1:47

Jesus is about to launch His earthly ministry and is in the process of recruiting disciples. Jesus sees Nathanael setting under a fig tree. But before Jesus introduces Himself to Nathanael, He declares that He knows the heart of Nathanael. What an awesome thought, that God knows the real you and sees things in you that you may not see yet.

The fact that God sees our heart should be the thing that motivates our direction, that changes our thoughts, that causes us to actually look at ourselves. The great bondage-breaking moment in our lives is when we learn to see ourselves as God sees us...as fearfully, uniquely, and wonderfully made. Consider that Jesus is telling you today that He knows your heart. Let that be your motivation for this day.

What is your prayer concerning what Jesus said to you?

_____

_____

_____

_____

_____

_____

_____

_____

_____

_____

Day 8

Give, and it will be given to you. They will pour into your lap a good measure, pressed down, shaken together, and running over. For by your standard of measure it will be measured to you in return.

—Luke 6:38

Imagine you have a bucket with things in it to give, and as you give the things in your bucket away you discover that your bucket grows larger with the same things you have given away.

In this great sermon, Jesus describes what it means to be a follower of Christ, given the standards, conducts, and attitudes. Jesus challenged His disciples to give, with a promise of an overflowing return. We should give what we wish to receive. We add to our lives by what we give from our lives.

Accept Jesus's challenge today and give love, grace, forgiveness, patience, etc., with an expectation of an overflowing return.

What is your prayer concerning what Jesus said to you?

_____

_____

_____

_____

_____

_____

_____

_____

_____

_____

Day 9

Truly, truly, I say to you, unless a grain of wheat falls into the earth and dies, it remains alone; but if it dies, it bears much fruit.

—John 12:24

The cycle of a seed dying then producing fruit is the natural process in nature. In this parable, Jesus is of course speaking of Himself. That through His death, He would produce much fruit in the lives of believers. We, being that fruit, now have the responsibility of continuing the process. If we are to be productive each day, we must die each day.

Follow Jesus's lead and crucify the tyrannical self-serving rule of self and let God's will, not our will, be done each day, that we in turn might produce much fruit.

What is your prayer concerning what Jesus said to you?

_____

_____

_____

_____

_____

_____

_____

_____

_____

_____

Day 10

Truly, truly, I say to you, the Son can do nothing of Himself, unless it is something He sees the Father doing; for whatever the Father does, these things the Son also does in like manner.

—John 5:19

There were those who wanted to harm Jesus because He called God His Father, and their concern was by doing so, He considered Himself equal to God. Jesus's response was that He could do nothing without His Father. He only did what He saw His Father doing, and whatever His Father does He does the same.

The world may dislike us as well for who we claim to be, but our response should be the same as Jesus. Jesus reminds us that on our own we can do nothing, but if we begin each day seeking what the Father is doing and join Him in like manner, all things are possible. If we live our lives daily seeking and doing the will of our Father, our haters will see our great works and marvel.

What is your prayer concerning what Jesus said to you?

_____

_____

_____

_____

_____

_____

_____

_____

_____

_____

Day 11

---

*The eye is the lamp of the body; so then if your eye is clear,
your whole body will be full of light. But if your eye is bad,
your whole body will be full of darkness. If then the light
that is in you is darkness, how great is the darkness!*

—Matthew 6:22–23

As Jesus shares with His disciples the true measure of wealth, He reminds them what we value the most will control our hearts. So He points them to spiritual insight.

The things we see are measured and valued based on either the world's perspective or God's perspective. Spiritual insight is the ability to see what God sees, to measure and assess value from God's viewpoint, which brings God's light into our lives. Jesus cautioned the disciples and us that if we allow our vision to be clouded by self-serving desires, interest, and goals, we will be full of darkness, with there being no limits to the darkness. So hear the words of Jesus and learn to keep our eyes clear with godly vision as we walk each day fully in the light of God.

What is your prayer concerning what Jesus said to you?

11

Day 12

*But seek first His Kingdom and His Righteousness,
and all these things will be added to you.*

—Matthew 6:33

The thing that causes worry and anxiety is when we have our priorities out of order. When we set achievements, people, and things as our priority, worry and anxiety are the natural results. Jesus points His disciples to nature—birds, flowers, grass—and reminds them of God's faithfulness of provisions in nature. We should have no worries or anxiety if we have trust in the things God has promised to supply (Phil. 4:19). Jesus directs His disciples and us to prioritize our days, seeking kingdom goals and the righteous things of God first, with the promise that the rest will fall into place.

What is your prayer concerning what Jesus said to you?

_____

_____

_____

_____

_____

_____

_____

_____

_____

_____

Day 13

If you love those who love you, what credit is that to you? For even sinners love those who love them.

—Luke 6:32

In this sermon to the disciples, Jesus begins with a series of blessings and cautions; blessings for those who committed to following Christ and cautions to those who only sought the things of the world. Jesus's call to His disciples was for them to be different in what they did, how they responded, and, most of all, in the way they loved. He reminded the disciples that there was no credit to them if they did what the world did and responded the way the world responded.

Jesus challenged the disciples and us to be different and make a difference by treating others the way we wanted to be treated, love the way God loved, and by that standard it would be measured back to us in return.

What is your prayer concerning what Jesus said to you?

_____

_____

_____

_____

_____

_____

_____

_____

_____

_____

_____

Day 14

Follow Me!

—Mark 2:14

As Jesus passed through Capernaum, He saw Levi (Matthew) and extended to him the invitation to follow Him. Levi, a man doing his daily job. It was a job despised by many, which led to a seedy reputation. But what we see is a man who, when invited to follow Jesus, did so without hesitation. In spite of his job, reputation, or knowledge of what it required, he followed.

Hear Jesus's voice as we face each day. He continuously invites us to follow Him. In spite of our jobs, our reputation with people, or complete knowledge, don't hesitate to follow...

What is your prayer concerning what Jesus said to you?

_____

_____

_____

_____

_____

_____

_____

_____

_____

Day 15

―――――――― ⟡ ――――――――

*These things I have spoken to you, so that in Me you
may have peace. In the world you have tribulation
but take courage; I have overcome the world.*

—John 16:33

As Jesus spoke to His disciples concerning their trust in His promises
and their belief in Him as coming from God, He also reminded them
that He would soon leave to go back to His Father. But though He
was leaving, He shared with them the importance of learning to trust
in His promises and believe in Him, for in doing so they would find
peace.

Jesus declares to the disciples and us that in this world we will
have our share of trials and tribulations, but if we lived what we
believed and trusted about Jesus, we will overcome, because He has
overcome.

What is your prayer concerning what Jesus said to you?

_____

_____

_____

_____

_____

_____

_____

_____

_____

_____

_____

Day 16

You give them something to eat.

—Luke 9:13

It had been recommended to Jesus, due to the isolated area and the size of the crowd, that they be sent into the surrounding villages to find lodging and food. But Jesus's response to the disciples was surprising. He recommended they feed them. The disciples of course felt overwhelmed by the size of the crowd and the lack of resources. Jesus saw an opportunity to teach the disciples, and us, that when He calls us to a task, don't get blinded by the size of the task or the lack of resources.

Because of the disciples' willingness to trust and obey Jesus, they had the opportunity to participate and experience the awesome power of God, the feeding of over five thousand people with only two fish and five loaves of bread. Listen to and obey Jesus's call today, and you too could experience a great move of God.

What is your prayer concerning what Jesus said to you?

_____

_____

_____

_____

_____

_____

_____

_____

_____

_____

Day 17

But who do you say that I am?

—Matthew 16:15

Jesus asked His disciples two questions. The first was, "Who do people say that I am?" The answer was a common view, that He was one of the great prophets. But the second and more important question was, "Who do you say I am?" The answer to that question would determine their relationship with God, the power that would reside in them for day-to-day living, and the security of their eternal hope.

If Jesus asked you this question, how would you answer? How you answer this question, who you believe and trust Him to be, will determine how you face and prevail each day of your life. So answer Jesus's question. Who do you say that He is?

What is your prayer concerning what Jesus said to you?

_____

_____

_____

_____

_____

_____

_____

_____

_____

_____

Day 18

Rightly did Isaiah prophesy of you hypocrites, as it is written: This people honor Me with their lips, but their heart is far away from Me.

—Mark 7:6

The Pharisees questioned Jesus about His disciples not following their traditions. Jesus responds to their question by calling them hypocrites. He charged them with being committed to their traditions but having no true devotion to God.

Each day we are called to know the word of God, understand the will of God, and to live a life that matches our love and devotion to God. As you hear Jesus's rebuke of these Pharisees ring in your ears, be certain that hypocrite has no place in your life. Honor God with your lips and your life.

What is your prayer concerning what Jesus said to you?

_____
_____
_____
_____
_____
_____
_____
_____
_____
_____

Day 19

Indeed, the very hairs of your head are all numbered. Do not fear; you are more valuable than any sparrows.

—Luke 12:7

The world will evaluate you based on how it thinks it knows you. They will assess your self-worth based on how you act, what you achieve, or how you look. But Jesus declares your value is based on the intimate details of how well God knows you as your Creator. As you move through life, do not allow your peers to determine your worth when God has already determined you are worth His Son's life. Hear Jesus declare your value and walk confidently in it.

What is your prayer concerning what Jesus said to you?

_____
_____
_____
_____
_____
_____
_____
_____
_____
_____

Day 20

I am no longer in the world; and yet they themselves are in the world, and I come to You. Holy Father, keep them in Your name, the Name which You have given to Me, that they may be one even as We are.

—John 17:11

As Jesus acknowledged that His departure from this world was nearing, He prays to His Father for those that He would leave behind. Jesus prays to the Father to keep them in His name. The name that kept Him, the name that raised Him, and the name that unified Them.

Find comfort and strength in this prayer for all believers left in this world. As you face each day, be reminded of Jesus's prayer that you have His name to protect you; you have the power in His name to raise you and the strength in His name to keep you as you grow in unity for the glory of God.

What is your prayer concerning what Jesus said to you?

_____

_____

_____

_____

_____

_____

_____

_____

_____

_____

Day 21

For what will it profit a man if he gains the whole world and forfeits his soul? Or what will a man give in exchange for his soul?

—Matthew 16:26

The accumulation of wealth, achievements, or status are all profitable. But Jesus cautioned the disciples to consider the cost. Jesus recommended that they live life with an eternal perspective. As you make life choices daily, consider Jesus's caution of the cost of the world's gain. Evaluate your life choices for its eternal purpose.

What is your prayer concerning what Jesus said to you?

_____

_____

_____

_____

_____

_____

_____

_____

_____

_____

Day 22

I am the way, the truth, and the life; no one
comes to the Father but through Me.

—John 14:6

Life can leave you with many questions. Which way do I go in life, what is the truth about life, and what is life? Jesus answered all these questions. Jesus declared that He is the path that led to the God of life, He is the truth concerning the God of life, and He is God in this present life.

Each day you should follow the clear path lead by Jesus, which is laid out by and with a consistent truth in the word of God, and live each day of your life in the very presence of God.

What is your prayer concerning what Jesus said to you?

_____

_____

_____

_____

_____

_____

_____

_____

_____

_____

Day 23

But many who are first will be last; and the last, first.

—Matthew 19:30

While most strived for riches, position, power, and fame, Jesus reminded the disciples that these things come with difficulties. That while the world's goal was to be on top, His order of things would be reversed. To be humbly committed in following Christ came with its own difficulties, but it also came with rewards both now and eternally. Each day as you humbly follow Christ, do so with no stress of the outcome but with the expectation that God would be reconstructing the order of things.

What is your prayer concerning what Jesus said to you?

_____
_____
_____
_____
_____
_____
_____
_____
_____
_____

Day 24

We must work the works of Him who sent Me as long as it is day; night is coming when no one can work.

—John 9:4

Ecclesiastes 11:4 says, "He who watches the wind will not sow, and he who looks at the clouds will not reap." The disciples were distracted with matters that were of no importance to Jesus. Jesus pointed them to the fact that He didn't have time to waste. There was work to be done. Our life is the limited time God has given us to do His work. As you consider the words of Jesus, each day should serve as a reminder that we too don't have time to waste. Make the most of each day that God gives.

What is your prayer concerning what Jesus said to you?

_____

_____

_____

_____

_____

_____

_____

_____

_____

_____

Day 25

But who do you say that I am?

—Luke 9:20

After feeding the five thousand, Jesus asked His disciples two questions. One was, "Who do people say that I am?" The disciples answered with various ideas. But the second question was more personal. He asked, "Who do you say that I am?" Peter answered that He was the Christ.

If Jesus asked you this question today, would your answer be the response of others, or would your life say that He was the Christ? Live each day in a way that shouts that He is the Christ and Lord of your life.

What is your prayer concerning what Jesus said to you?

_____
_____
_____
_____
_____
_____
_____
_____
_____
_____

Day 26

My food is to do the will of Him who sent
Me and to accomplish His work.

—John 4:34

The disciples were concerned about Jesus's physical needs, which was food for His body. But Jesus was more focused on His spiritual needs. While the disciples urged physical nourishment for Jesus, Jesus informed them that His nourishment was to do and complete the will of the Father. As you begin a new day, what is your priority, physical or spiritual? Hear the words of Jesus and make the Father's will your priority.

What is your prayer concerning what Jesus said to you?

_____

_____

_____

_____

_____

_____

_____

_____

_____

Day 27

My Father, if it is possible, let this cup pass from Me; yet not as I will, but as You will.

—Matthew 26:39

Many times, our feelings can cloud our decisions. Jesus finds Himself in the Garden of Gethsemane agonizing and hurt by what He was facing, His impending crucifixion. Jesus in His human nature did what most do when filled with emotions and tough decisions. He asked God to relieve Him of the pain and from the tough decision. But He overcame His emotions and surrendered to the will of God.

As you face each day with its many decisions and hurtful circumstances, follow the example of Jesus by making decisions centered in the will of God over your emotions.

What is your prayer concerning what Jesus said to you?

_____
_____
_____
_____
_____
_____
_____
_____
_____
_____
_____

Day 28

Having eyes, do you not see? And having ears, do you not hear? And do you not remember?

—Mark 8:18

The disciples began to discuss among themselves their lack of provisions among them. Jesus questioned their hearts, asking them about what they had seen and heard while in His presence.

As you approach each day, there may be times you feel as though you are ill-equipped or lack the provisions to carry on. Jesus calls you to remember what you've seen Him do and the profound truths He has shared in your walk with Him. Jesus is reminding you to watch and listen; He always provides in abundance.

What is your prayer concerning what Jesus said to you?

_____

_____

_____

_____

_____

_____

_____

_____

_____

Day 29

Do you not yet understand?

—Mark 8:21

Jesus had just reminded the disciples of the things He had done and the abundant outcome. He then questioned their understanding. Sometimes we are so overwhelmed by our situation or circumstance that we miss what God has done or is doing. Maybe even spiritual or physical blessings become so routine that we fail to see or understand what God is doing.

Take time each day to search for understanding of what God is saying or doing in and through your life. Hear the voice of Jesus asking, "Do you understand?"

What is your prayer concerning what Jesus said to you?

_____

_____

_____

_____

_____

_____

_____

_____

_____

_____

Day 30

If anyone wishes to come after Me, he must deny himself,
and take up his cross daily and follow Me.

—Luke 9:23

After the feeding of the five thousand, it would not be out of the realm of possibility that many would follow Jesus simply because of the miraculous provision just recently provided. But Jesus shares with the disciples what it would require to be a true follower of Him. Jesus says it will require personal denial and a sacrificial commitment. As you approach each day, be sure you are not following for the fish and bread (provisions and blessings) but are truly committed to following Christ.

What is your prayer concerning what Jesus said to you?

_____

_____

_____

_____

_____

_____

_____

_____

_____

_____

Red-Letter Day Devotional

Praise God, from whom all blessings flow. You have completed the first thirty days of the *Red-Letter Day Devotional.* I pray that you have enjoyed these first thirty days of intimately hearing and sharing with Jesus as you journaled your response to what He has shared with you. I have been praying from the beginning of writing this devotional that you would get the same sense of warmth, intimacy, and comfort I received as I spent each day hearing from and talking to Jesus.

As you begin the next thirty days, my prayer for you, of course, is that the intimacy would grow deeper with even more dependency on hearing from and talking to Jesus each day. To do that you may need to carve out a little more time for your devotional time. The reason for this is that the first thirty days you journaled your response to my commentary of the Scriptures, but in these next thirty days, you will be journaling your own commentary of what Jesus says to you in the passage of Scripture and continue journaling your response to what Jesus says to you.

This may seem difficult at first, but reread the passage, read more scripture for context, pray for clarity, and, if necessary, use other commentary, but give your own commentary as to what Jesus says to you. As you continue this daily conversation with Jesus, you'll find it becoming easier each day. This will become possible because you will develop a sensitive ear for Jesus and a growing intimacy with Him.

As you begin these last thirty days, know that I have already prayed for you, that each devotional day will become so significant and special that you can't wait for the next. Begin these next thirty days with great expectation of what Christ will share with you and the change He will make in you.

Let's get started!

Day 31

With people this is impossible, but with God all things are possible.

—Matthew 19:26

What is Jesus saying to you?

_____
_____
_____
_____
_____
_____
_____
_____
_____
_____

What is your prayer concerning what Jesus said to you?

_____
_____
_____
_____
_____
_____
_____
_____
_____
_____

Day 32

You do not want to go away also, do you?

—John 6:67

What is Jesus saying to you?

_____

_____

_____

_____

_____

_____

_____

_____

_____

_____

What is your prayer concerning what Jesus said to you?

_____

_____

_____

_____

_____

_____

_____

_____

_____

_____

Day 33

That which proceeds out of the man, that is what defiles the man.

—Mark 7:20

What is Jesus saying to you?

_____
_____
_____
_____
_____
_____
_____
_____
_____
_____

What is your prayer concerning what Jesus said to you?

_____
_____
_____
_____
_____
_____
_____
_____
_____
_____

Day 34

Do not worry then, saying, What will we eat? or What will we drink? or What will we wear for clothing?

—Matthew 6:31

What is Jesus saying to you?

_____
_____
_____
_____
_____
_____
_____
_____

What is your prayer concerning what Jesus said to you?

_____
_____
_____
_____
_____
_____
_____
_____
_____

Day 35

*So do not worry about tomorrow; for tomorrow will care
for itself. Each day has enough troubles of its own.*

—Matthew 6:34

What is Jesus saying to you?

_____

_____

_____

_____

_____

_____

_____

_____

_____

What is your prayer concerning what Jesus said to you?

_____

_____

_____

_____

_____

_____

_____

_____

_____

Day 36

*Which of these three do you think proved to be a neighbor
to the man who fell into the robbers' hands?*

—Luke 10:36

What is Jesus saying to you?

_____
_____
_____
_____
_____
_____
_____
_____
_____

What is your prayer concerning what Jesus said to you?

_____
_____
_____
_____
_____
_____
_____
_____

Day 37

My Father is working until now, and I Myself am working.

—John 5:17

What is Jesus saying to you?

_____
_____
_____
_____
_____
_____
_____
_____
_____

What is your prayer concerning what Jesus said to you?

_____
_____
_____
_____
_____
_____
_____
_____
_____

Day 38

Follow Me!

—Mark 2:14

What is Jesus saying to you?

_____

_____

_____

_____

_____

_____

_____

_____

_____

_____

What is your prayer concerning what Jesus said to you?

_____

_____

_____

_____

_____

_____

_____

_____

_____

_____

Day 39

He who has ears to hear, let him hear.

—Mark 4:9

What is Jesus saying to you?

_____

_____

_____

_____

_____

_____

_____

_____

_____

_____

What is your prayer concerning what Jesus said to you?

_____

_____

_____

_____

_____

_____

_____

_____

_____

_____

Day 40

*The harvest is plentiful, but the laborers are few; therefore, beseech
the Lord of the harvest to send out laborers into His harvest.*

—Luke 10:2

What is Jesus saying to you?

_____
_____
_____
_____
_____
_____
_____
_____
_____
_____

What is your prayer concerning what Jesus said to you?

_____
_____
_____
_____
_____
_____
_____
_____
_____

Day 41

The one who listens to you listens to Me, and the one who rejects you rejects Me; and he who rejects Me rejects the One who sent Me.

—Luke 10:16

What is Jesus saying to you?

_____
_____
_____
_____
_____
_____
_____
_____
_____
_____

What is your prayer concerning what Jesus said to you?

_____
_____
_____
_____
_____
_____
_____
_____
_____
_____

Day 42

※

*How can you say you believe, when you receive glory from one another
and you do not seek the glory that is from the one and only God?*

—John 5:44

What is Jesus saying to you?

_____

_____

_____

_____

_____

_____

_____

_____

_____

_____

What is your prayer concerning what Jesus said to you?

_____

_____

_____

_____

_____

_____

_____

_____

_____

_____

Day 43

It is I; do not be afraid.

—John 6:20

What is Jesus saying to you?

_____

_____

_____

_____

_____

_____

_____

_____

_____

_____

What is your prayer concerning what Jesus said to you?

_____

_____

_____

_____

_____

_____

_____

_____

_____

_____

Day 44

Do not work for the food which perishes, but for the food which endures to eternal life, which the Son of Man will give to you, for on Him the Father, God, has set His seal.

—John 6:27

What is Jesus saying to you?

_____

_____

_____

_____

_____

_____

_____

_____

_____

What is your prayer concerning what Jesus said to you?

_____

_____

_____

_____

_____

_____

_____

_____

_____

Day 45

Ask, and it will be given to you; seek, and you will find; knock, and it will be opened to you.

—Matthew 7:7

What is Jesus saying to you?

_____

_____

_____

_____

_____

_____

_____

_____

_____

_____

What is your prayer concerning what Jesus said to you?

_____

_____

_____

_____

_____

_____

_____

_____

_____

_____

Day 46

In everything, therefore, treat people the same way you want
them to treat you, for this is the Law and the Prophets.

—Matthew 7:12

What is Jesus saying to you?

_____
_____
_____
_____
_____
_____
_____
_____
_____
_____

What is your prayer concerning what Jesus said to you?

_____
_____
_____
_____
_____
_____
_____
_____
_____
_____

Day 47

A lamp is not brought to be put under a basket, is it or under a bed? Is it not brought to be put on the lampstand?

—Mark 4:21

What is Jesus saying to you?

_____

_____

_____

_____

_____

_____

_____

_____

_____

_____

What is your prayer concerning what Jesus said to you?

_____

_____

_____

_____

_____

_____

_____

_____

_____

_____

Day 48

Take Care what you listen to. By your standard of measure, it will be measured to you; and more will be given you besides.

—Mark 4:24

What is Jesus saying to you?

_____

_____

_____

_____

_____

_____

_____

_____

_____

_____

What is your prayer concerning what Jesus said to you?

_____

_____

_____

_____

_____

_____

_____

_____

_____

_____

Day 49

Blessed are the eyes which see the things you see.

—Luke 10:23

What is Jesus saying to you?

_____
_____
_____
_____
_____
_____
_____
_____
_____
_____

What is your prayer concerning what Jesus said to you?

_____
_____
_____
_____
_____
_____
_____
_____
_____
_____

Day 50

Martha, Martha, you are worried and bothered about so many things...

—Luke 10:41

What is Jesus saying to you?

_____

_____

_____

_____

_____

_____

_____

_____

_____

_____

What is your prayer concerning what Jesus said to you?

_____

_____

_____

_____

_____

_____

_____

_____

_____

_____

Day 51

I am the bread of life; he who comes to Me will not hunger, and he who believes in Me will never thirst.

—John 6:35

What is Jesus saying to you?

_____

_____

_____

_____

_____

_____

_____

_____

_____

_____

What is your prayer concerning what Jesus said to you?

_____

_____

_____

_____

_____

_____

_____

_____

_____

_____

Day 52

My time is not yet here, but your time is always opportune.

—John 7:6

What is Jesus saying to you?

_____

_____

_____

_____

_____

_____

_____

_____

_____

_____

What is your prayer concerning what Jesus said to you?

_____

_____

_____

_____

_____

_____

_____

_____

_____

_____

Day 53

Truly I say to you, I have not found such great faith with anyone in Israel.

—Matthew 8:10

What is Jesus saying to you?

_____

_____

_____

_____

_____

_____

_____

_____

_____

_____

What is your prayer concerning what Jesus said to you?

_____

_____

_____

_____

_____

_____

_____

_____

_____

_____

Day 54

But go and learn what this means: I desire compassion, and not
sacrifice, *for I did not come to call the righteous, but sinners.*

—Matthew 9:13

What is Jesus saying to you?

_____

_____

_____

_____

_____

_____

_____

_____

_____

_____

What is your prayer concerning what Jesus said to you?

_____

_____

_____

_____

_____

_____

_____

_____

_____

_____

Day 55

Go home to your people and report to them what great things the Lord has done for you, and how He had mercy on you.

—Mark 5:19

What is Jesus saying to you?

_____

_____

_____

_____

_____

_____

_____

_____

_____

_____

What is your prayer concerning what Jesus said to you?

_____

_____

_____

_____

_____

_____

_____

_____

_____

_____

Day 56

For whoever wishes to save his life will lose it, but whoever
loses his life for My sake and the gospel's will save it.

—Mark 8:35

What is Jesus saying to you?

_____
_____
_____
_____
_____
_____
_____
_____
_____
_____

What is your prayer concerning what Jesus said to you?

_____
_____
_____
_____
_____
_____
_____
_____
_____
_____

Day 57

*On the contrary, blessed are those who hear
the word of God and observe it.*

—Luke 11:28

What is Jesus saying to you?

_____

_____

_____

_____

_____

_____

_____

_____

_____

_____

What is your prayer concerning what Jesus said to you?

_____

_____

_____

_____

_____

_____

_____

_____

_____

_____

Day 58

If therefore your whole body is full of light, with no dark part in it, it will be wholly illumined, as when the lamp illumines you with its rays.

—Luke 11:36

What is Jesus saying to you?

_____
_____
_____
_____
_____
_____
_____
_____
_____
_____

What is your prayer concerning what Jesus said to you?

_____
_____
_____
_____
_____
_____
_____
_____
_____
_____

Day 59

I am the Light of the world; he who follows Me will not walk in the darkness, but will have the Light of life.

—John 8:12

What is Jesus saying to you?

_____
_____
_____
_____
_____
_____
_____
_____
_____
_____

What is your prayer concerning what Jesus said to you?

_____
_____
_____
_____
_____
_____
_____
_____
_____
_____

Day 60

The thief comes only to steal and kill and destroy; I came that they may have life and have it abundantly.

—John 10:10

What is Jesus saying to you?

_____
_____
_____
_____
_____
_____
_____
_____
_____
_____

What is your prayer concerning what Jesus said to you?

_____
_____
_____
_____
_____
_____
_____
_____
_____
_____

The Conclusion

Blessed is the man who does not walk in the counsel of the wicked, nor stand in the path of the sinner, nor sit in the seat of the scoffer! But his delight is in the law of the LORD, and in His law, he meditates day and night. He will be like a tree firmly planted by the streams of water, which yields its fruit in its season, and its leaves do not wither; and in whatever he does, he prospers.

—Psalms 1:1–3

Blessed sets the tone for the man who delights in hearing, meditating on, and applying the Word of God. Nothing provides more motivation, instruction, or direction than God's Word. It is the resource for strength, prosperity, and success in the midst of tough times. You have just completed sixty days of hearing from and responding to Jesus. Blessed should be the outcome. The blessings you should be experiencing are as follows: New Chapters, Renewed Faith, and New Results.

New Chapters

This is the day which the LORD has made;
let us rejoice and be glad in it. (Psalms 118:24)

Each year is an accumulation of months, weeks, and days. You can't get to a year, a month, or a week without first getting through a day. The psalmist reminds us to celebrate each day. Each day is a new page in the New Chapter of life. Yesterday is a distant memory, and tomorrow is a prayer, but if we spend time each day with God celebrating each day, blessed are you.

Jesus reminds us not to worry about tomorrow, "for tomorrow will care for itself. Each day has enough trouble of its own" (Matt. 6:34). Many of the struggles I experienced in the year 2020 was due to worrying about what would happen tomorrow; what's next? Jesus's emphasis was the same as the psalmist; celebrate the day, live in the moment with Him, and let tomorrow take care of itself.

Through my daily conversations with Jesus, I could see myself building on each day as I developed this new chapter in my life. I pray you too have recognized through these past sixty days the strength, courage, and motivation in your life as you spent each day with Jesus. As you celebrate each day building a new chapter, rejoice and be glad in what God is doing in and through your life. Continue to let God write your new chapter!

Renewed Faith

And we know that God causes all things to
work together for good to those who love God,
to those who are called according to His purpose.
(Romans 8:28)

As I spent each day with Jesus, I could sense His faithfulness, His love, and His patience. What was lacking was my faith in Him to work it out. Jesus tells us that He came that we would have life and have it in abundance. What we bring to the table of abundance is our trust in and application of His word. The only way to "know" is to trust, to spend quality time with Him. To witness Him work not just in isolated situations but to do it in all things.

Our love for God is shown through our knowledge and application of God's word (i.e., obedience). Each day we spend knowing and understanding the will of God, His purpose becomes our purpose with the understanding/faith that there is a promised, positive outcome.

Through these past sixty days, I pray you've noticed the call to hear what Jesus said and pray concerning what He has said. Too often we don't take the time to hear what God has to say, and simply tell Him what we want Him to do. For sixty days, we've had a central focus: hear what Jesus is saying and respond to what Jesus says. Why? Because we build faith when we know and understand what God is telling us, so we pray with confidence (i.e., faith) knowing that God will work it out for good. My prayer for you is that you recognize the growth of your faith and continue to build and renew your faith as you continue to hear and respond to God.

New Results

> And without faith it is impossible to please Him, for he who comes to God must believe that He is a rewarder of those who diligently seek Him. (Hebrews 11:6)

I realized during this period of struggle that simply acknowledging that I believed in the existence of God was not enough. I've spent a large portion of my life acknowledging God's existence, but I have since learned that it is in the struggles of life that we realize how intimate our relationship is. To many that I've counseled who are going through struggles, I would ask the question, have you prayed about it? Often the answer would be "I don't know what to pray." Some have even noticed that their prayers are shallow or simply mimic what they've heard others pray. This is clearly an indication of a lack of intimacy.

Through these sixty days of hearing from and responding to Jesus, you should have sensed the intimacy, and in the intimacy, dependency. In my quality time with God, I've learned the benefits/rewards of diligently seeking Him. The results were a growing intimacy, faith, and dependency on Him. It was through my intimacy that I developed my dependency, which made it clear I couldn't please Him without faith/trust. The word of God clearly implies that for our new chapter and renewed faith to produce new results, we need to, by faith, diligently seek quality time with God. I pray that these sixty days have set you on that course.

The Conclusion

> And inasmuch as it is appointed for men to die once and after this comes judgment, so Christ also, having been offered once to bear the sins of many, will appear a second time for salvation without reference to sin, to those who eagerly await Him. (Hebrews 9:27–28)

The Word of God reminds us that our lives are time-stamped. That at the conclusion of our lives, our life will be judged by the only true Judge. These verses remind us that if we commit our lives to seeking to hear from and responding to God and because of the life and death of Jesus, our judgment will be "Well done, My good and faithful servant."

I don't know, or ever will know, when or how the end will come, but here is what I do know; I can trust God to write each chapter of my life, and I can trust Him with the results. So I eagerly await Him. I challenge you to do the same.

> All scripture is inspired by God and is profitable for teaching, for reproof, for correction, for training in righteousness; so that the man/ woman of God may be adequate, equipped for every good work. (2 Timothy 3:16–17)

I chose the words of Jesus for this sixty-day devotional. This passage of scripture reminds us that all of God's Word is profitable if we spend time knowing, understanding, and applying it. We began this devotional describing a red-letter day, denoted as a day that is pleasantly noteworthy, memorable, or of special significance. We concluded with the fact that any day that starts with talking to and/

or hearing from God would be noteworthy, memorable, special, and significant. So, by definition, any day can be a red-letter day if we use any of God's Word to hear from and respond to God.

I pray that you will continue your own daily devotional, using any and all of Scripture to make all of your days red-lettered. Using the last thirty days as a template, continue your daily devotional, to assure yourself of being adequate and equipped for every good work.

I wrote this devotional as a way of paying it forward for what the Lord did for me in the midst of my struggles in 2020. My prayer for you is, if this sixty-day devotional has helped you in any way, you will pay it forward as well, by investing in someone's life, a spouse, family member, friend, coworker, or church member, by gifting them a copy of this *Red-Letter Day Devotional*. This gift may lead to their personal revival. It did for me.

God bless!

About the Author

James W. Reed III is a graduate of Jarvis Christian College of Hawkins, Texas, and the proud pastor of Rising Sun Baptist Church in Beaumont, Texas. He has been in ministry for over twenty-five years. He has a passion for God and evangelistic compassion for mankind. He considers himself an equipper of the saints. He teaches that spiritual growth consists of knowledge, understanding, and the application of the Word of God. The Bible commands that we grow in knowledge, but without understanding, the application can be misguided. He believes that ministry is the call of every believer to participate in reconciling mankind back to God.

Lightning Source UK Ltd.
Milton Keynes UK
UKHW050919190822
407499UK00006B/222

9 798885 405300